How Can Gun Violence Be Stopped?

Other titles in the *Issues Today* series include:

How Can Gun Violence Be Stopped?

Carla Mooney

ReferencePoint
Press®

San Diego, CA

For more information, contact:
ReferencePoint Press, Inc.
PO Box 27779
San Diego, CA 92198
www.ReferencePointPress.com

LIBRARY OF CONGRESS CATALOGING-IN-PUBLICATION DATA

Names: Mooney, Carla, 1970- author.
Title: How can gun violence be stopped? / by Carla Mooney.
Description: San Diego, CA : ReferencePoint Press, [2021] | Series: Issues today | Includes bibliographical references and index.
Identifiers: LCCN 2020013033 (print) | LCCN 2020013034 (ebook) | ISBN 9781682828779 (library binding) | ISBN 9781682828786 (ebook)
Subjects: LCSH: Gun control--United States. | Firearms ownership--United States. | Firearms accidents--United States. | Violent crimes--United States.
Classification: LCC HV7436 .M66 2021 (print) | LCC HV7436 (ebook) | DDC 363.330973--dc23
LC record available at https://lccn.loc.gov/2020013033
LC ebook record available at https://lccn.loc.gov/2020013034

Dying from Gun Violence

The day began like any other Saturday in El Paso, Texas. On August 3, 2019, many people were shopping early before temperatures climbed into the hundreds. The local Walmart was a popular destination, attracting thousands of customers each day from El Paso and neighboring Juárez, Mexico. On this August weekend, many shoppers browsed in the store's back-to-school section located near one of the store's two entrances.

Around 10:30 a.m., store manager Robert Evans was taking a break outside the store. As he walked back inside, he heard what sounded like a loud backfire from a car. Evans turned around and spotted a man with a semiautomatic rifle in the parking lot. The gunman fired the weapon multiple times as he headed toward the store's entrance. Evans watched in horror as several people were hit by bullets. "Once I saw more rounds coming out, and these people dropping, I proceeded back into the store," Evans says. He grabbed his two-way store radio and sent an emergency alert to other employees that an act of violence was in progress. As the gunman entered the store, Evans hustled customers toward a rear exit while trying to call 911 from his cell phone. "It seemed like forever. It seemed like it'd never stop," Evans says. "I was shaking and breathing heavily [with] adrenaline, running to get everyone out of the building. . . . There are no words."[1]

Meanwhile, inside the Walmart, Octavio Ramiro Lizarde, a twenty-three-year-old construction worker from El Paso, stood in line at the in-store bank with his fifteen-year-old nephew Javier Amir Rodriquez. Suddenly, he heard gunshots. As the store erupted in chaos, Lizarde tried to hide with Rodriquez in the bank manager's office. However, before they could reach the office, the shooter appeared and shot them both. Rodriquez was killed outright. "I did lose my nephew right in front of me," Lizarde says. "It was a horrible image and I hope nobody ever goes through it. It's very painful."[2]

In only a few minutes, the El Paso shooting became one of the deadliest mass shootings in modern US history. Twenty-two people were killed, and nearly two dozen others were injured in the attack. Shortly after the shootings, the gunman, twenty-one-year-old Patrick Crusius of Allen, Texas, surrendered without a fight to El Paso police about a block away from the Walmart. Two months before the shooting, Crusius had legally purchased the semiautomatic rifle and one thousand rounds of ammunition online. Then, in August, he drove eleven hours from his home outside of Dallas, Texas, to El Paso with the intent of killing immigrants and Mexicans. Crusius was charged with capital murder in Texas and could face the death penalty if convicted. In addition, he was indicted on ninety federal charges, including hate crimes. He could face the death penalty on each of the federal charges linked to the people who were killed and up to life in prison for the charges relating to the wounded victims.

A Bigger Problem

Mass shootings like the one in El Paso dominate headline news and capture the public's attention. Each time a mass shooting event occurs, intense discussions about the need to stop gun violence reignite across the country. Calls for gun reforms and safety measures increase. Yet while mass shootings are highly publicized, they are only one piece of the gun violence puzzle in the United States.

Gun violence includes all gun-related homicides and suicides. Recent statistics show the extent of gun violence in the United States. In 2017, the most recent year for which complete data is available from the Centers for Disease Control and Prevention (CDC), 39,773 people died from gun-related injuries in the United States. Of those deaths, 60 percent were suicides and 37 percent

Rate of US Gun Deaths Rises Over Time

According to a 2019 Pew Research Center report, in 2017 the United States experienced its highest rate of gun deaths in more than two decades. The 2017 rate was 12 gun deaths per 100,000 people. While the overall rate is lower than the highest rate in 1974, when there were 16.3 gun deaths per 100,000 people, there is still a trend that shows both gun murders and gun suicide rates increasing in recent years.

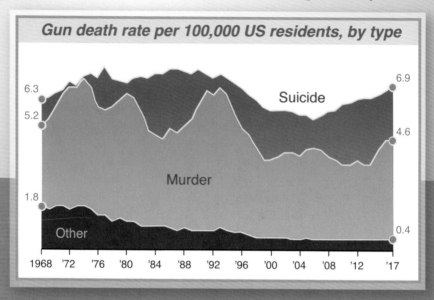

Gun death rate per 100,000 US residents, by type

Suicide

6.3

5.2

6.9

4.6

Murder

1.8

Other

0.4

1968 '72 '76 '80 '84 '88 '92 '96 '00 '04 '08 '12 '17

Note: "Other" includes gun deaths that were unintentional, involved law enforcement, or had undertermined circumstances.

Source: John Gramlich, "What the Data Says About Gun Deaths in the U.S.," Pew Research Center, August 16, 2019. www.pewresearch.org.

were murders. A small number of gun-related deaths (3 percent) were the result of unintentional shootings, involved law enforcement, or had undetermined circumstances.

In addition, the rate of gun-related deaths in the United States is much higher than in many other countries, according to researchers at the Institute for Health Metrics and Evaluation at the University of Washington. In a study that compared the gun-related death rates of 195 countries and territories published in 2018, the United States ranked twentieth with 10.6 deaths per 100,000 people in 2016, the most recent year in the study. Although this rate was lower than several Latin American countries, it was higher than most developed nations, including Canada (2.1 deaths per 100,000), Australia (1.0), France (2.7), and Germany (0.9). In addition, the study found that more than 250,000 people died from gun-related injuries worldwide in 2016. More than half of those deaths occurred in only six countries: Brazil, the United States, Mexico, Colombia, Venezuela, and Guatemala. "This study confirms what many have been claiming for years—that gun violence is one of the greatest public health crises of our time," says Mohsen Naghavi, a professor of global health at the institute and the lead author of the study. "There are no simple antidotes to address this health problem. The tragedy of each firearm-related death will continue until reasonable and reasoned leaders come together to address the issue."[3]

> "Gun violence is one of the greatest public health crises of our time."[3]
>
> —Mohsen Naghavi, a professor of global health at the Institute for Health Metrics and Evaluation, University of Washington

The Debate over How to Reduce Gun Violence

While most people agree that gun violence in all forms needs to be stopped, there is intense debate over the best way to achieve that goal. Guns are deeply ingrained in American history and society. Since the country's founding, the Second Amendment to the US Constitution gives Americans the right to bear arms. For many Americans, this right is a part of daily life. According to an October 2019 Gallup poll, 40 percent of American adults have a gun in their home or on their property. Americans own guns for personal safety, hunting, recreation, and other reasons. Most gun owners view owning guns as part of their personal freedoms as Americans and oppose limits on their ability to own guns.

At the same time, many people are calling for gun control measures to reduce gun violence. Proposals for increased legislation of gun sales and ownership, required licensing, and bans on certain types of guns are some of the measures being debated. Roger Marmet is one of many people who marched in Washington, DC, to spread awareness about gun violence in communities across America. Marmet has directly experienced the devastation of gun violence. His twenty-two-year-old son, Tom, was killed by a bullet while sitting in his car in Washington, DC, in 2018. Marmet believes change is needed to prevent more tragic gun-related deaths. "It's not even safe to just drive across town, and we have to do something about it,"[4] he says.

CHAPTER ONE

Should Assault-Style Weapons Be Banned?

In the past decade, shooters with assault-style weapons have launched deadly attacks in public places, including schools, churches, and movie theaters. On October 2, 2017, a gunman opened fire on a large crowd enjoying a country music festival in Las Vegas. The gunman, sixty-four-year-old Stephen Paddock from Mesquite, Nevada, had checked into a nearby hotel several days earlier. Using twenty-three guns, some of which were upgraded with bump stocks that allowed them to fire in rapid succession, Paddock fired at the crowd from his hotel room window at 10:05 p.m. Within ten minutes, he discharged more than eleven hundred rounds of ammunition. He killed fifty-eight people and injured more than eight hundred others in the deadliest mass shooting in US history. Paddock killed himself before police could take him into custody, and his motives for the shooting remain unclear.

On February 14, 2018, Nikolas Cruz entered Marjory Stoneman Douglas High School in Parkland, Florida, and opened fire with his legally purchased AR-15 semiautomatic rifle. Cruz shot rapid streams of bullets through hallways, shattering windows and shooting through doors. In less than four minutes, he killed seventeen people and wounded seventeen others. Cruz ditched his rifle and exited the school in a crowd of escaping students. Later that day, police tracked him down and arrested him. He was charged with seventeen counts of first-degree murder and seventeen counts of attempted murder. His killing spree remains the deadliest high school shooting in US history.

After a 2018 mass shooting at Marjory Stoneman Douglas High School in Parkland, Florida, people throughout the United States grieved for the victims, and students countrywide participated in protests for gun control.

Calls to Ban Assault-Style Weapons

The deadly mass shootings in Las Vegas, Parkland, and other places have fueled public outcry over assault-style weapons. Gun control advocates argue that this type of gun, which is often the type of weapon used in mass shootings, increases the number of casualties. They have renewed calls for an outright ban on these types of weapons, but gun rights activists oppose such measures.

Currently, there is no federal ban on assault-style weapons, high-capacity magazines, or bump stocks. Assault-style weapons are civilian versions of weapons originally designed for the military. During the 1980s, the gun industry attempted to increase consumer demand for guns by developing new types of weapons based on military designs. It developed guns that allow shooters to fire large amounts of ammunition very quickly while maintaining control of the gun. For example, an AR-15 semiautomatic rifle, like the one used in the Parkland shootings, can fire up to forty-five rounds per minute. An AK-47 semiautomatic rifle, like the one used in the El Paso shooting, can fire hundreds of rounds per minute.

Assault-style weapons are designed to kill quickly and efficiently. In addition, the wounds caused by assault-style weapons are often more severe and lethal than wounds caused by other guns. For these reasons, assault-style weapons are often the guns of choice for shooters planning to carry out a mass shooting attack. According to a 2019 analysis of public mass shootings from 1981 to 2017 that resulted in four or more deaths, more than 85 percent of fatalities in these shootings were caused by assault-style rifles. Another 2018 study found that a shooter with an assault-style rifle can hurt and kill twice the number of people as a shooter armed with a standard rifle or handgun can.

Devices such as high-capacity magazines and bump stocks further increase the ability of assault-style weapons to harm large numbers of people quickly. High-capacity magazines hold more ammunition, which allows shooters to fire more rounds without stopping to reload. A bump stock combines two legal devices: a plastic stock and a gun. When paired together, they allow the gun to operate at a rate of fire comparable to a fully automatic machine gun. In the Las Vegas shooting, the gunman attached a bump stock to twelve of his semiautomatic rifles, which allowed them to fire faster.

Gun control advocates insist that assault-style weapons were originally manufactured for military use and have no place in the

March for Our Lives

In March 2018, the survivors of the deadly school shooting in Parkland, Florida, which killed seventeen students and faculty members, organized the March for Our Lives demonstrations in support of legislation to prevent gun violence in the United States. The rally took place in Washington, DC, with more than eight hundred coordinated events throughout the country and the world. Across the United States, 1.2 to 2 million people attended these events, making it one of the largest protests in US history. "Those 17 people did not die in vain," said seventeen-year-old Casey Sherman, a Parkland survivor and one of the student organizers. "We will stop at nothing until we make real, lasting change."

Quoted in New York Times, "March for Our Lives Highlights: Students Protesting Guns Say 'Enough Is Enough,'" March 24, 2018. www.nytimes.com.

hands of civilians. They point out that the Las Vegas shooter and other recent mass shooting killers were able to walk into a gun shop and legally purchase their assault-style weapons after passing a standard background check. If a federal assault weapons ban had been in place, they would not have been able to buy the deadly guns. In a 2019 op-ed in the *New York Times*, former vice president Joe Biden called for banning assault-style weapons:

> Shooters looking to inflict mass carnage choose assault weapons with high-capacity magazines capable of holding more than 10 rounds. They choose them because they want to kill as many people as possible without having to stop and reload. In Dayton, [Ohio,] where the police responded immediately and neutralized the shooter within about 30 seconds, he was still able to massacre nine people and injure more than two dozen others because he carried an AR-style weapon with a magazine capable of holding 100 rounds. We have to get these weapons of war off our streets.[5]

Many Americans agree with the need for a federal ban on assault-style weapons. According to an August 2019 poll by Morning Consult and Politico, 70 percent of polled voters supported a ban on assault-style weapons. In addition, 72 percent of those polled supported banning high-capacity magazines.

However, others oppose a ban. Gun rights organizations such as the National Rifle Association (NRA) argue that most owners of these types of guns are law-abiding citizens. Banning these weapons would be in violation of citizens' Second Amendment

"Shooters looking to inflict mass carnage choose assault weapons. . . . They choose them because they want to kill as many people as possible without having to stop and reload. . . . We have to get these weapons of war off our streets."[5]

—Joe Biden, the forty-seventh US vice president

In a 2019 op-ed in the New York Times, *former vice president Joe Biden (pictured) called for a ban on assault-style weapons.*

rights. Gun rights advocates also point out that enforcement of a ban would be extremely challenging because millions of guns and magazines are already owned by citizens. They also argue that a ban on assault-style weapons would do little to significantly reduce gun violence because the majority of gun-related violence is committed with handguns, which would not be covered by the ban.

The 1994 Federal Ban

In 1994, Congress passed and President Bill Clinton signed the Violent Crime Control and Law Enforcement Act of 1994 into law. A subsection of the act prohibited the manufacture or sale of certain semiautomatic weapons for civilian use. The act also banned high-capacity magazines that could hold ten rounds or more.

In order to get the votes needed to pass the act, the ban's sponsors agreed to a grandfather clause that allowed those who already owned assault-style weapons to keep their guns. In addition, those who owned grandfathered-in weapons before the ban were still allowed to legally sell the guns to others. Legislators also accepted a provision under which the 1994 ban would automatically expire in ten years unless Congress voted to renew it. In 2004, the ban expired and has not been reinstated.

Was the Ban Effective?

Since its expiration, the effectiveness of the assault-style weapons ban has been debated. One of the most-cited studies on the ban's effectiveness was completed in 2004. The report by the National Institute of Justice found that the number of gun crimes involving semiautomatic weapons decreased by 17 percent during the ban in six cities reviewed in the study. However, the report stated that it was premature to make any conclusions about the ban's effectiveness and noted that any benefits from the ban were likely to be offset by the use of nonbanned firearms.

In 2018, the RAND Corporation undertook a comprehensive review of gun laws and their impact on gun use. RAND found that

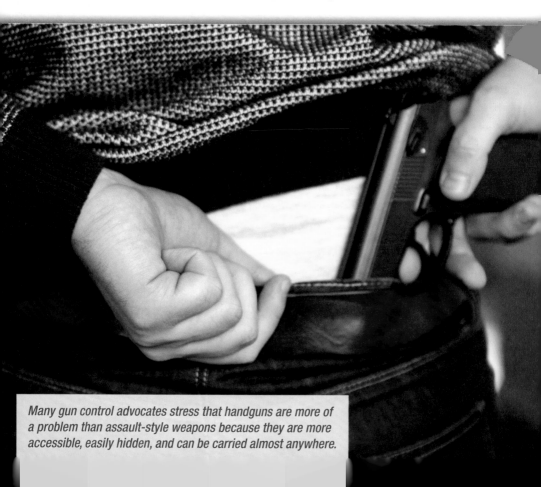

Many gun control advocates stress that handguns are more of a problem than assault-style weapons because they are more accessible, easily hidden, and can be carried almost anywhere.

existing studies were either inconclusive or showed only limited evidence that bans on the sale of assault-style weapons were effective at reducing crime and mass shootings.

One reason why the federal ban on assault-style weapons may have had a minimal effect on reducing gun violence is that this type of gun was used in only a small number of shootings across the country. According to the RAND report, most gun-related crimes are committed with handguns, which are not considered assault weapons. For example, the RAND analysis noted that only 252 (2.6 percent) of the 9,616 gun-related murders in 2015 that it reviewed involved any type of rifle.

Anton Bell, the commonwealth's attorney in Hampton, Virginia, agrees that handguns are more of a problem than assault weapons in incidents of gun violence. "The overwhelming majority of firearms that we deal with are handguns," says Bell. "They're more accessible. They are easily hidden, and the key to a lot of the crimes is being able to bring these guns anywhere. With the handguns, you can conceal them and they [will] not be detected. . . . And we absolutely have far too many illegal handguns on the street."[6] According to Federal Bureau of Investigation (FBI) statistics from 2016, only 3.4 percent of gun-related homicides were committed with rifles and 2.4 percent with shotguns.

However, some studies have found that criminal use of assault weapons had begun to decrease right before the ban expired. "By the time the ban was lifted in 2004, we were starting to see a decrease in criminal use of assault weapons and high-capacity magazines," says Christopher Koper, a George Mason University criminologist. He suggests that a ban on assault weapons and

"The overwhelming majority of firearms that we deal with are handguns. They're more accessible. They are easily hidden, and the key to a lot of the crimes is being able to bring these guns anywhere."[6]

—Anton Bell, the commonwealth's attorney in Hampton, Virginia

Bump Stock Ban

In March 2019, a federal ban on bump stocks, which are gun attachments that allow shooters to fire a semiautomatic rifle continuously with only one pull of the trigger, went into effect. The US Department of Justice determined that bump stocks were covered under an existing ban of fully automatic weapons. Owners of bump stocks were given ninety days to turn in or destroy their bump stocks. Because registration of bump stocks is not required, Justice Department officials do not know the exact number of bump stocks owned by private citizens, but they estimate the number to be in the tens of thousands. While gun control advocates applaud the ban, gun rights groups have had mixed reactions. The NRA expressed its disappointment that a grandfather clause was not included that would allow people who had purchased bump stocks when they were legal to keep them. Other groups, such as the Gun Owners of America, have promised to challenge the ban in court.

high-capacity magazines might not be a quick fix to reduce gun violence but rather a longer-term policy. "It might take some time to get the desired effects,"[7] Koper says.

Researchers have also found that in the years since the ban expired, criminal use of semiautomatic weapons fitted with large detachable magazines has increased in many cities. According to a 2017 study published in the *Journal of Urban Health*, high-capacity semiautomatic weapons increased from 33 to 112 percent as a share of the types of guns used in crimes during the years after the ban expired.

When looking specifically at the ban's impact on mass shootings, researchers found the ban did make a difference in mass shooting events. Louis Klarevas, a research professor at Teachers College of Columbia University, has collected data on every mass shooting—which he defines as an event in which six or more people are shot and killed—from 1966 to 2016. He looked to see if the ten-year federal ban on assault weapons had any impact on mass shootings. Klarevas found that the number of gun massacres during the ban fell by 37 percent when compared to the ten-year period before the ban.

Not only did the number of mass shootings decrease, but the number of people killed in them also decreased by 43 percent. After the ban expired in 2004, the numbers increased again: mass shootings increased by 183 percent, and deaths in mass shootings increased by 239 percent. Klarevas believes that the ban on high-capacity magazines that could hold more than ten rounds was a key part of the 1994 ban. "We have found that when large capacity mags are regulated, you get drastic drops in both the incidence of gun massacres and the fatality rate of gun massacres,"[8] he says. A 2019 study published in the *Journal of Trauma and Acute Care Surgery* also reported a similar result. Compared to the decades before and after the ban, mass shooting fatalities were 70 percent less likely during the federal ban period.

> "We have found that when large capacity mags are regulated, you get drastic drops in both the incidence of gun massacres and the fatality rate of gun massacres."[8]
>
> —Louis Klarevas, a research professor at Columbia University's Teachers College

Renewed Efforts to Pass a Federal Ban

In January 2019, a group of senators led by Dianne Feinstein of California and Chris Murphy and Richard Blumenthal of Connecticut introduced a new bill, the Assault Weapons Ban of 2019. The bill aims to ban the sale, transfer, manufacture, and importation of military-style assault weapons and high-capacity magazines. "Military-style assault rifles are the weapons of choice for mass murderers. There's just no reason why these guns, which were designed to kill as many people as quickly as possible, are sold to the public,"[9] says Murphy. A similar bill was also introduced in the US House of Representatives in February 2019.

As of February 2020, both the House and Senate bills had stalled in committee and appeared unlikely to be passed. Representative David Cicilline of Rhode Island, the primary sponsor of the House bill, admits that it has been difficult to get the support needed to pass such a ban because it goes further than restricting gun access to felons and the mentally ill. "Let's be honest," says Cicilline. "Every other bill that we've done tries to keep guns out of the hands of people who shouldn't have them. This is the one piece of legislation that keeps a particular weapon out of the hands of law-abiding citizens. A lot of people have enormous objections to that."[10]

State Bans on Assault-Style Weapons

Without a federal ban on assault-style weapons, some states have passed their own legislation to ban them. Currently, seven states—California, Connecticut, Hawaii, Maryland, Massachusetts, New Jersey, and New York—and Washington, DC, ban certain types of assault-style weapons. In addition, nine states and Washington, DC, ban high-capacity magazines. In some cases, the state laws are stricter than the 1994 federal ban. For example, California, Connecticut, Hawaii, New Jersey, and New York require that owners register assault-style weapons that were legally purchased before the state bans were enacted. Several states also prohibit such owners from selling or transferring these guns to another person.

However, little research has been done on the effectiveness of state assault-style weapons bans. Mark Gius from Quinnipiac University is one of the few researchers who has studied the data from state assault weapon bans. His research found that although state bans did not reduce gun homicides in general, they were associated with a decrease in mass shooting fatalities.

State bans may be less effective than a federal ban because it is easy for a shooter to legally purchase an assault-style weapon in one state and then use it in another state. In July 2019, nineteen-year-old Santino William Legan opened fire at the Gilroy Garlic Festival, located about 30 miles (48 km) south of San Jose, California. He used an AK-47 assault-style rifle to kill three people and injure at least twelve others. Although this type of weapon is banned and not sold in California, Legan was able to legally purchase the gun a few weeks earlier in Nevada, which does not have a state assault weapons ban. "I can't put borders up . . . in a neighboring state where you can buy this damn stuff legally," says California governor Gavin Newsom. "I have no problem with the Second Amendment, you have a right to bear arms but not weapons of . . . mass destruction."[11]

> "I have no problem with the Second Amendment, you have a right to bear arms but not weapons of . . . mass destruction."[11]
>
> —Gavin Newsom, the governor of California

In addition, states that have implemented bans often face widespread noncompliance from gun owners. A New York law passed in 2013 banned the sale of all new assault weapons and required mandatory registration with state police of all grandfathered weapons that were already owned by residents. However, only about 45,000 of an estimated 1 million guns were registered eighteen months after the law was passed. Attorney and policy analyst Paloma Capanna believes that the noncompliance is based on widespread opposition to mandatory registration. "It's not that they aren't aware of the law," says Capanna. "The lack of registration is a massive act of civil disobedience by gun owners statewide."[12]

Is a Ban Enough?

Many people believe that banning assault-style weapons will go a long way toward reducing gun violence and reducing the devastating casualties in mass shooting events. However, others point out that most gun-related deaths and injuries do not involve these weapons. Therefore, they argue that banning these guns will only take away the rights of law-abiding citizens while having little impact on overall gun violence in America.

CHAPTER TWO

Should Universal Background Checks Be Required for All Gun Purchases?

On August 31, 2019, thirty-six-year-old Seth Aaron Ator shot a police officer who had pulled him over for a traffic stop on a highway that connects Midland and Odessa, Texas. As he fled police and drove toward Odessa, Ator hijacked a postal truck and fired at civilians. As the police hunted for Ator, businesses, offices, and the local university in Odessa were put on lockdown.

Junior Bejarano was working at a restaurant in Odessa when he heard a gunshot outside. "It was chaos in a matter of seconds," he says. "People were screaming, flipping chairs, dropping plates." A few minutes later, Bejarano and other workers stepped outside the restaurant and saw several cars at a nearby intersection with bullet holes. Inside one of the cars, a young child was shot. "She was conscious, but she was just covered in blood," Bejarano says. "It was horrible to see something like that."[13]

Ator killed seven people and injured at least twenty-two others before police were able to shoot and kill him. The investigation into the deadly rampage revealed that Ator had previously failed a criminal background check to buy firearms. "Not only did the Odessa gunman have a criminal history . . . he also previously failed a gun purchase background check in Texas," tweeted Texas governor Greg Abbott in the days after the shootings.

"(And) he didn't go thru a background check for the gun he used in Odessa."[14] Instead, Ator bought his rifle in a private person-to-person sale. In Texas, private sales do not require background checks, and Ator was able to buy his gun without one.

Gun control advocates point out that the Odessa tragedy could have been avoided if the federal government required universal background checks for all gun sales and closed the loophole for private sales. John Feinblatt, the president of the organization Everytown for Gun Safety, was one of many who called on Congress to act quickly. "This is exhibit A of the deadliness of the background check loophole. This weekend alone, seven Americans are dead after a preventable mass shooting, because the Senate has refused to require background checks on all gun sales," he said in a statement after the shooting. "Americans are tired of excuses: The time for Senate action on background checks is now, and Americans will not be fooled by a weak, ineffective legislative response."[15]

> "Americans are tired of excuses: The time for Senate action on background checks is now."[15]
>
> —John Feinblatt, the president of Everytown for Gun Safety

Federal Background Checks

Background checks for gun purchases are intended to prevent prohibited people—such as convicted felons, minors, drug users, those with a history of mental illness, those subject to a restraining order, and those convicted of domestic violence—from having access to guns. Currently, the United States does have a federal background check law. Passed in 1994, the Brady Handgun Violence Prevention Act requires federally licensed gun dealers to conduct background checks on every person who wants to purchase a gun by using the FBI's National Instant Criminal Background Check System (NICS). Federally licensed gun dealers include gun stores, retail stores, and pawn shops. By restricting access to guns for people who have been determined to be dangerous, the law aims to reduce gun crime and violence. In

A 1998 amendment to federal firearm legislation made it legal for dealers to sell guns to individuals who had not passed a background check if the process was delayed and dealers were not notified of the delay.

2018 alone, more than 26 million background checks were performed prior to gun purchases, and nearly one hundred thousand gun sales were blocked.

The act originally required a five-day waiting period before a person could take possession of a handgun. In 1998, the legislation was amended to eliminate the waiting period. In addition, if an individual did not pass a background check after three days and the government had not notified the dealer to explain the delay, the person in question could purchase a gun.

Private Sale Loopholes

However, critics point out that there are large loopholes in the current federal law. Gun sales between private sellers and buyers do not require a background check. Private sales, which occur online, at gun shows, and person-to-person, can all be done without a federal license or a background check. Private sellers are defined as individuals who do not rely on selling guns as their primary livelihood.

According to a 2017 study by researchers at Northeastern University and Harvard University, one in five US gun owners had obtained a firearm during the previous two years without having a background check. The study also found that states that did not regulate private gun sales had a significantly larger percentage of gun sales between private sellers and buyers (57 percent) as compared to states that did regulate private sales (26 percent). The study's results show that millions of Americans acquire guns each year without background checks. "Our research makes the case for the adoption of laws in states that do not currently regulate private firearm transfers," says Matthew Miller, the study's lead author and a professor of health sciences and epidemiology in Northeastern's Bouvé College of Health Science. "And

Incomplete Records Lead to Tragedy

On November 5, 2017, Devin Patrick Kelley opened fire in a church in Sutherland Springs, Texas. In the shooting, he carried an assault-style rifle and two handguns, which he used to shoot and kill twenty-six people. Although he had a known record of domestic violence, Kelley passed a background check and was able to buy the guns himself. In 2012, while he was in the US Air Force, Kelley was court-martialed for assaulting his wife and stepson and served a year in confinement at a naval facility after a plea bargain. However, this conviction never surfaced in the background check performed when he bought his guns. An investigation after the shooting revealed that his domestic violence offense was not entered into the federal database used for gun purchase background checks. The case highlights one of the flaws of the background check system: voluntary record submissions from law enforcement agencies are often incomplete or inadequate. "We could build the best IT (information technology) system money can buy—the fastest, most efficient," says Stephen Morris, a former assistant FBI director who oversaw the FBI's background check operation in West Virginia. "In the end, it is only as good as the information that is fed into it. Like they say: Garbage in, garbage out."

Quoted in Kevin Johnson, "Texas Church Shooting: Background Check Breakdown Highlights Federal Gun Record Problems," *USA Today*, November 9, 2017. www.usatoday.com.

it underscores the fact that we're talking about millions of gun transfers annually that pass from one private owner to another without a formal vetting process and so without knowing whether the recipient is someone society deems a lawful possessor of firearms."[16]

Because of the private sale loophole, people who are likely to commit gun violence can easily obtain firearms from the unregulated gun market without background checks. Interviews with people convicted of gun crimes have found that few purchase guns from licensed retailers. Instead, they get guns through underground sellers or informal networks that can sell or transfer guns without oversight or background checks.

Jody Lee Hunt was banned by federal law from owning a gun because he was a felon who had served time in prison for the abduction of a previous girlfriend. However, when he wanted to buy a gun, he had little trouble doing so. Hunt bought a handgun from

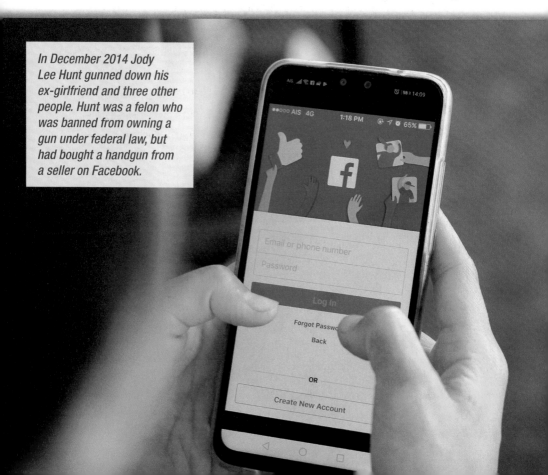

In December 2014 Jody Lee Hunt gunned down his ex-girlfriend and three other people. Hunt was a felon who was banned from owning a gun under federal law, but had bought a handgun from a seller on Facebook.

a private seller on Facebook. In December 2014, he used that handgun in a deadly attack in West Virginia in which he killed his ex-girlfriend, a rival business owner, and two other people before shooting himself.

States Closing the Loophole

Several states have attempted to close the private sale loophole in federal laws by requiring that background checks be performed for all firearm sales and transfers, including those that occur between private sellers. These laws are known as universal background check laws. For example, California requires all gun sales, including private transactions, to go through a firearms dealer that has been licensed by the state. In addition, purchases of shotguns, rifles, and handguns are subject to a fifteen-day waiting period to make sure all gun buyers undergo and pass a thorough background check before purchasing a gun. According to the Giffords Law Center to Prevent Gun Violence, twenty-one states and Washington, DC, have added background check legislation for at least some private sales. Like California, several states require universal background checks for all firearm sales and transfers. Other states, including Pennsylvania, require background checks for all handgun sales but not for rifles and shotguns. Some states, such as Hawaii and Massachusetts, require all firearm buyers to get a permit, which can only be issued after passing a background check, before they buy any gun.

Some research has found that state universal background checks have helped reduce gun violence. A 2019 study led by researchers at Boston University's School of Public Health concluded that states with laws that required universal background checks for all gun sales had homicide rates that were 15 percent lower than states without universal background checks. Researchers say the study results show that universal background checks are effective at reducing gun violence. "Research has shown that the greatest risk factor for violence is a history of violent behavior," explains lead study author Michael Siegel, a professor of community health sciences. "Public health advocates should prioritize policies designed to keep guns out of the hands of people who are at a high risk of violence based on their criminal history,"[17] he says.

In some states, the effectiveness of universal background check laws has been less clear. A study published in 2017 in the medical journal *Injury Prevention* found that the enactment of state universal background check laws did little to increase the number of background checks performed in Colorado and Washington. The researchers suggest that implementation and enforcement of the law may have been issues in these states. When the laws were initially passed, opponents in Colorado and Washington publicly voiced their intent not to comply with the new laws. In Washington, more than one thousand supporters of gun rights held a demonstration at the state capital with the slogan "I will not comply." In Colorado, some sheriffs in rural areas were reported as saying they either would not enforce the background check law or would make enforcement a very low priority.

"We know background check laws work," says Sarah Tofte, research director at Everytown for Gun Safety. "This research also shows how critical implementation and enforcement are, and it suggests Colorado and Washington still have gaps in those areas that can and should be addressed."[18] Josh Horwitz, the executive director of the Coalition to Stop Gun Violence, agrees and warns that it can take years to see positive results from universal background check laws. "Passing these laws is just part of the battle, and making sure they work effectively once they're passed is very, very important," says Horwitz. "It really takes time for the system to coalesce around the new law, and that's because people have done things one way for a long time."[19] In addition, because people can easily travel from one state to another, they can circumvent state laws by purchasing guns in a state that does not require checks and then transporting them across state lines.

Federal Universal Background Checks

Gun control advocates point out that current federal background check laws with private sale loopholes and the patchwork of state laws make it easy for potentially violent people to get their hands on a dangerous firearm. They urge the federal government to implement and enforce a strong universal background check law to make it harder for criminals, domestic abusers, the mentally ill, and others at risk of violence to access guns. Keeping guns out of the hands of those most likely to use them violently is essential to reducing gun violence. Many Americans support the passage of federal universal background check laws. According to a July 2019 poll by NPR, *PBS NewsHour*, and Marist College, 89 percent of Americans surveyed said they supported background checks for all gun purchases, including those at gun shows, online, and in other private sales.

In February 2019, the US House of Representatives passed a bill that would require federal universal background checks. The bill mandates background checks on all gun sales, including private firearm sales. There are some exceptions, however. Background

One Step Closer to a Gun Registry

Gun rights advocates believe that implementing universal background checks will bring Americans one step closer to a national gun registry. Some, like John Whitehead of the Rutherford Institute, are concerned that the existence of a national gun registry would make it easier for the federal government to confiscate privately owned firearms. "If there is a centralized system with information relating to firearm possession," he says, "it becomes much easier for governments at all levels to seize firearms when it suits them. A centralized registry allows not only federal law enforcement, but state and local as well, to quickly and efficiently deprive lawful owners of their guns if they feel there is some emergency justifying it."

Quoted in Travis Dunn, "Would Universal Background Checks Create National Gun Registry?," WhoWhatWhy .org, April 8, 2019. https://whowhatwhy.org.

checks would not be required for transfers between close relatives or to lend a gun to someone for use at a shooting range or for hunting. "Background checks work," Representative Mike Thompson of California, the lead Democratic author on the bill, said on the House floor. "Every day, they stop 170 felons and 50 domestic abusers from getting a gun from a licensed dealer. But, in some states, those same people can go into a gun show or go online and buy a gun without a background check. This bill will help stop them from doing so."[20]

Gun rights advocacy groups, such as the NRA, oppose the bill. They argue that widening the databases that can be searched as part of the NICS is a better idea than expanding background checks. "This extreme gun-control bill will make criminals out of law-abiding Americans. It will also make it harder for good people to defend themselves and their families," says Chris W. Cox, the executive director of the NRA's legislative arm. "Criminals, on the other hand, will continue to get their firearms the way they always have—through the black market, theft and straw purchases. Forcing more government paperwork and additional fees on good people trying to exercise a constitutional right will do nothing to make Americans safer."[21] As of early 2020, the House bill had stalled in the Senate.

"This extreme gun-control bill will make criminals out of law-abiding Americans. It will also make it harder for good people to defend themselves and their families."[21]

—Chris W. Cox, the executive director of the NRA's legislative arm

Not Always Effective

Opponents of universal background checks point out that even when these laws are implemented, they do not always work to prevent gun violence. A background check is only as good as the records available. If background data in the NICS is incomplete or mislabeled, a person who should not be able to buy a gun could pass the background check and buy a gun.

A gun shop worker looks at paperwork for a customer's background check. If background data is incomplete or mislabeled, someone who should not be eligible to buy firearms could pass the background check and buy a gun anyway.

On June 17, 2015, twenty-one-year-old Dylann Roof killed nine people in a South Carolina church using a gun he never should have been allowed to buy. Roof had previously been arrested for drug possession. This history should have surfaced on a background check and stopped him from buying a gun. However, Roof's background check got held up without a decision. Under federal law, the FBI has three business days to determine whether there is enough cause to deny a gun purchase to an individual. If the agency cannot come to a decision within that period, the buyer can legally go ahead and purchase the gun. Because of this loophole, Roof was able to legally buy the handgun that he used in the killing spree.

The majority of Americans support the idea of universal background checks to keep guns out of the hands of people who are most likely to use them for violence. However, as evidenced by tragedies such as South Carolina's 2015 church shooting, the background check system is not foolproof. Even when background checks are required, errors in the system and loopholes in the law allow violent people access to deadly firearms.

CHAPTER THREE

Should the Government Expand Gun Ownership Regulations?

Many activities and jobs in the United States, from driving and fishing to teaching and cutting hair, are regulated by the government. Yet in many states, there are few regulations on gun ownership. Some people propose that expanding gun ownership regulations is one way to reduce gun violence. Expanded regulations can take several forms, including licensing requirements, additional restrictions on who qualifies to own guns, and emergency provisions that allow law enforcement to remove guns from owners who are determined to be at an elevated risk of gun violence. Not all of these are popular, though, with those who fear such restrictions on gun rights.

Licensing Laws

In the United States, every person must pass a test in order to obtain a driver's license, which legally allows an individual to drive. Yet for guns, there are no federal regulations that require a person to obtain a license to purchase or possess a gun. At the state level, only thirteen states and Washington, DC, require gun owners to obtain a license to own or possess firearms. "For the most part, it is much easier to be a legal gun owner in America than it is to be a legal driver,"[22] says David Hemenway, the director of the Injury Control Research Center at the Harvard T.H. Chan School of Public Health.

Licensing laws have been shown to be effective at ensuring that guns are only bought and used by responsible adults. When a permit to purchase or license to own a gun is required, a person typically must complete a background check and an in-person application at a police station or other law enforcement agency. In addition to a background check, the in-person application acts as another safeguard to prevent dangerous people from obtaining guns.

> "For the most part, it is much easier to be a legal gun owner in America than it is to be a legal driver."[22]
>
> —David Hemenway, the director of Harvard's Injury Control Research Center

Some licensing laws require gun owners to maintain a valid license and periodically renew the license, just like a driver's license. Required renewals help law enforcement reconfirm that a person is eligible to own a gun. If a gun owner becomes ineligible because of criminal conviction or another reason, law enforcement is alerted to confiscate that firearm. In addition, gun licensing laws can improve safe and responsible gun ownership. Some laws require applicants to complete a safety training course and firearm safety tests to demonstrate that buyers and owners know gun laws and how to safely load, fire, and store a gun.

Studies show that gun licensing laws can effectively reduce gun-related homicides and suicides. According to a 2019 paper published by researchers at the Johns Hopkins Center for Gun Policy and Research, states with gun licensing laws experience less gun violence than states without licensing laws. For example, researchers found that after Connecticut implemented its gun licensing law in 1995, gun-related homicides dropped by 40 percent and gun-related suicides decreased by 15 percent over ten years. In contrast, when Missouri repealed its gun licensing law in 2007, the state experienced increases in gun-related homicides of 17 to 27 percent through 2017.

An instructor observes a trainee during a firearms class. Some states have laws that require prospective gun buyers to complete a safety training course and firearm safety tests before they are allowed to purchase a firearm.

The Johns Hopkins researchers say their study shows that requiring a license to buy a gun is even more effective than background checks at reducing gun violence. "There is good evidence showing that when states augment CBC [comprehensive background check] laws with mandatory licensing or permitting of handgun purchasers, lives are saved by lower rates of firearm-involved homicides and suicides." The researchers explained their findings, writing that

requiring that applicants be fingerprinted and apply to law enforcement for a license requires intention and planning over a matter of days, providing time for the potential impulse buyer to change his or her mind. This built-in waiting period allows for transitory feelings to pass and reduces the chance of purchasers using the gun to harm them-

selves or others. This is particularly relevant for firearm suicide since many attempts occur within minutes or hours of
deciding to make the attempt.[23]

In addition, licensing laws may reduce straw purchases, which
occur when one person buys a gun for a prohibited person or
someone who does not want his or her name linked to the gun
purchase. Requiring the purchaser to meet in person with law
enforcement officials to obtain a license can act as a deterrent to
straw purchases.

Most of the American public supports the implementation of
licensing laws for gun ownership. A 2019 survey by Quinnipiac
University found that 77 percent of Americans polled said they
supported a law that required a person to get a license from a
law enforcement agency before being able to purchase a firearm.

Expanding Restrictions on Gun Ownership

Another proposal for reducing gun violence is expanding existing restrictions on who can legally possess a firearm. Currently,
federal law prohibits the purchase and possession of guns by
certain people, such as convicted felons, domestic abusers, and
people with a history of specific kinds of mental illness. However,
federal law does not ban other questionable groups of people
from purchasing firearms even though public health researchers
have identified these groups as having a significantly higher risk of
becoming violent as compared to the general population.

Currently, under federal law, a person who has been convicted
of a felony crime or a misdemeanor domestic violence offense
cannot purchase a gun. However, a person who has been convicted of another type of misdemeanor crime, even if it is violent
or involved a firearm, can still buy a gun. Yet studies have shown
that people who have already committed a violent crime are much
more likely to commit future violent acts. According to the Giffords
Law Center, research shows that a person with a conviction for
a violent misdemeanor is nine times more likely to commit future
violent crimes and nine times more likely to commit future firearm

Research has shown that people who have committed a violent crime are much more likely to commit future violent acts. But in all states except California, violent offenders can still legally purchase guns.

offenses. Other groups of people with a higher likelihood of becoming violent include people with a history of drug or alcohol abuse, people convicted of juvenile offenses, and people who have suffered from certain types of severe mental illness. Therefore, some argue that expanding gun restrictions to prevent people with violent histories from getting access to guns could help reduce gun violence.

The Hate Crime Gap

Bigotry and hate have fueled some of the deadliest mass shootings in the nation, from the June 12, 2016, Orlando nightclub shooting targeting the LGBTQ community to the October 27, 2018, Pittsburgh synagogue shootings. Yet these highly publicized mass shootings are only a small portion of the violent hate crimes involving guns that occur each year. With studies showing that hate crimes are on the rise, gun control advocates also support banning people who have committed hate crimes from owning guns. Currently, federal law bans any person convicted of a felony hate crime from buying and owning guns. Yet this ban does not include people convicted of misdemeanor hate crimes.

Researchers with the Center for American Progress have found that "individuals who commit hate crimes tend to escalate their conduct in order to ensure their message is received by the targeted individual or community." The researchers suggest that "keeping guns out of the hands of individuals who perpetrate hate crimes is therefore a crucial measure to help ensure the safety of groups that have historically been targeted because of their race, ethnicity, national origin, religion, gender, gender identity, sexual orientation, or disability." They conclude that "new legislation to prohibit individuals convicted of misdemeanor hate crimes from buying and possessing guns would not stop every hate-motivated shooting. It would, however, be a strong step toward keeping guns out of the hands of individuals who have proven themselves to be uniquely dangerous to historically vulnerable communities."[24]

Several state and federal bills have been introduced to keep guns out of the hands of those convicted of hate crimes. In 2017, California passed a state law that prohibits people who are convicted of misdemeanor hate crimes from purchasing and possessing guns within ten years of their conviction. "There are too many examples in our country's recent history, which show what a firearm can do in the hands of people who practice hate,"[25] says Los Angeles assemblyman Reggie Jones-Sawyer, who supported the law. Other states are debating similar legislation. In September 2019, the US House of Representatives considered the Disarm Hate Act, which would prohibit individuals who have been convicted of a misdemeanor-level hate crime from buying or possessing guns. "The link between gun violence and bigotry is clear. Convicted hate criminals are a danger to our society. They should not be allowed to legally own guns,"[26]

"The link between gun violence and bigotry is clear. Convicted hate criminals are a danger to our society. They should not be allowed to legally own guns."[26]

—David Cicilline, a representative from Rhode Island

Gun Purchase Bans Should Be Expanded

April Zeoli, an associate professor of criminal justice at Michigan State University and a gun control advocate, argues that dating partners should be included in laws prohibiting gun purchases:

> Under the federal law, I could be the victim of domestic violence and go for a domestic violence restraining order and get one. And if it were my husband that I was getting the restraining order against, he would have a firearm restriction on him. Now, I could have the exact same circumstances of domestic violence and go to get a domestic violence restraining order and get one, but if it is my boyfriend, that I never lived with, married, or had a child with, he would not have a firearm restriction on him. This is important because recently, it looks like just under half of intimate partner homicides are committed by dating partners. So by not putting this firearm restriction on dating partners, we are missing a population that we know commits domestic violence and we know commits fatal domestic violence.

Quoted in Kimberly Lawson, "How Closing the 'Boyfriend Loophole' in Gun Laws Could Save Lives," *Vice*, November 7, 2017. www.vice.com.

says Representative David Cicilline, who sponsored the bill. As of early 2020, no further action had been taken on the bill.

Close the Boyfriend and Stalker Gaps

Research shows that the combination of intimate partner violence and access to guns can be deadly. However, gaps in federal law allow domestic abusers and stalkers to obtain guns. Currently, federal law prohibits convicted domestic abusers from obtaining guns only if their crimes were against certain victims, such as spouses, parents, the other parent of a child, and a current or former cohabitant. Yet people who have been convicted of abusing a current or former girlfriend or boyfriend are not banned from buying or possessing guns. This "boyfriend gap" allows domestic abusers to access guns, which they can use against dating partners. In addition, although domestic abusers who have a

Gun Purchase Bans Go Too Far

Jennifer Baker, a spokesperson for the NRA, argues against expanding the federal ban on buying and possessing firearms to include dating partners convicted of domestic abuse and stalkers:

> [For] many of those "offenses"—and I'm using air quotes here—the behavior that would qualify as a stalking offense is often not violent or threatening; it involves no personal contact whatsoever. . . . Like if you were sending harassing messages to somebody on Facebook, to somebody you never met or somebody you dated five years ago. How it's written right now, you could be convicted for a misdemeanor stalking offense for a tweet that causes someone emotional distress and then you would be prohibited from owning a firearm.

Quoted in Sheryl Gay Stolberg, "Why the N.R.A. Opposes New Domestic Abuse Legislation," *New York Times*, April 1, 2019. www.nytimes.com.

permanent restraining order against them cannot legally own or buy guns, those who are only subject to a temporary order are not banned.

Another predictor of future violence is stalking behavior. Research has found that most women who were murdered or survived a murder attempt by a current or former partner were stalked during the year before the murder or murder attempt. Under current federal law, people convicted of misdemeanor stalking crimes are not prohibited from buying or possessing guns. As a result, gun control advocates support legislation that would close the "stalker gap" and prevent all people convicted of any type of stalking offense from buying guns.

To address these gaps in federal law, several states have passed laws to restrict access to guns and ammunition for domestic abusers. "A lot of people who commit domestic violence are dating partners, they're not in relationships that are recognized under federal law as domestic relationships, and therefore those abusers are not prohibited from purchasing or possessing firearms," says Allison Anderman, managing attorney at the

Giffords Law Center. "It's left up to the state to close that loophole."[27] In 2018, Oregon joined twenty-three other states in passing legislation to prohibit the purchase and possession of guns by convicted domestic abusers who dated their victims but did not live together or have a child together.

Not everyone agrees with Oregon's new gun restrictions. Kevin Starrett, head of the Oregon Firearms Federation, argues that the bill opens the door for false allegations of domestic abuse. "What this bill does is give people a mighty tool to destroy the life of an innocent person," he says. In addition, Starrett believes the restrictions will do little to reduce gun violence. "We think it's a farce that anyone believes a woman is protected from someone who is really dangerous by any piece of paper or the confiscation of guns,"[28] he says.

Under federal law, people who have been convicted of domestic abuse against dating partners are still legally able to buy firearms—including those with temporary restraining orders against them.

Extreme Risk Protection Orders

Sometimes a person who is thinking about harming themselves or others displays warning signs that family, friends, and coworkers observe. When these individuals have access to a gun, even if purchased legally, they become a greater danger. Extreme risk laws, also called red flag laws, enable families and law enforcement to petition a court directly for an extreme risk protection order (ERPO). An ERPO temporarily bans a person in crisis, with an elevated risk of harming themselves or others, from buying or possessing guns. An ERPO also requires the person to turn over any guns he or she already has while the order is in effect. These orders allow law enforcement to help people in crisis, reduce the risk of gun violence, and save lives.

In 2018, twenty-year-old Dakota Reed from Monroe, Washington, posted on Facebook that he wanted to commit a mass shooting at a synagogue and kill thirty Jewish people. He also posted pictures of himself with firearms, selfies of himself in a Nazi salute, and other hateful social media posts. After being tipped off about Reed, local officers obtained an ERPO and removed an assault weapon and eleven other guns from his home. Reed was arrested and charged with two counts of threats to bomb or injure property.

An ERPO can also reduce gun-related suicides by taking weapons out of the hands of those showing an elevated risk of self-harm. In one example, a man threatened to kill himself and his three-year-old son because he was increasingly frustrated over not being able to afford his child support payments. Law enforcement obtained an ERPO and temporarily removed ten guns, including assault weapons, from the man's home.

Extreme risk laws also may help prevent future school shootings. In 2018, a Maryland teenager, Luis Cabrera, threated on social media to open fire on his former high school. He wrote that he hoped everyone at the school died and posted pictures of himself holding semiautomatic rifles. The weapons legally belonged to a resident of the apartment where he lived. When students alerted law enforcement to the social media postings, the police obtained an ERPO and removed the guns from Cabrera's possession. Police also arrested the eighteen-year-old and charged him with making a threat of mass violence.

As of early 2020, seventeen states and Washington, DC, have enacted red flag laws. The laws allow police, friends, and relatives to report those whom they believe are at risk of harming themselves or others to authorities. A judge decides whether to grant the ERPO so that police officers can temporarily seize the firearms. The people at risk can challenge the petition in court and can petition for the guns to be returned after the risk of harm passes. Because an ERPO is considered a civil action, it does not leave the person at risk with a criminal record.

Two states with the earliest red flag laws, Connecticut (1999) and Indiana (2005), have experienced a decline in suicides after enacting the laws. According to a 2018 study from researchers at the University of Indianapolis, the gun-related suicide rate dropped 13.7 percent in Connecticut and 7.5 percent in Indiana in the subsequent ten-year period. Jeff Swanson, a professor of psychiatry at Duke University who has studied patterns of violence, notes that red flag laws may have their greatest impact in preventing suicides. "It's far more likely to be helping your young son or your granddad thinking about taking their own life" than preventing a mass shooting, he says. These laws "can be a doorway from a dark place."[29]

Preventing people who are at a higher risk of committing a violent act with a gun from getting access to firearms is one way to reduce gun violence. Proposals such as requiring licensing and safety training, expanding ownership restrictions, and implementing emergency provisions to remove guns from people in crisis have the potential to keep the public safer and reduce the tragedies caused by guns.

CHAPTER FOUR

Should Americans Be Able to Carry Guns in Public?

On the morning of Sunday, December 29, 2019, a gunman drew a shotgun and fired inside a crowded church in White Settlement, Texas. In only a few seconds, he killed two people and injured three others. He was stopped from harming others by two armed parishioners who, as part of the church's security volunteers, drew their own guns and killed him. "This team responded quickly and within six seconds the shooting was over. Two of the parishioners who were volunteers on the security force drew their weapon and took out the killer immediately—saving an untold number of lives," says Texas lieutenant governor Dan Patrick. "Had the shooter been able to indiscriminately start firing into the parishioners sitting there in front of him or the pastor, we would have had many more lives lost today and many more serious injuries."[30]

The incident set off debate over the role of guns in public. Gun rights advocates have long asserted that allowing law-abiding citizens to carry guns in public serves as a strong deterrent to gun violence. They argue that criminals are less likely to draw a gun if they know that others nearby are also armed. In addition, as shown in the Texas church shooting, armed citizens can quickly intervene as soon as a shooter opens fire, which can minimize casualties. However, not everyone agrees with this position. Some argue that allowing citizens to carry guns in public will instead increase the risk of gun violence.

A Texas church shooting in December 2019 ignited a debate over the role of guns in public places. Gun rights advocates claim that law-abiding citizens carrying guns in public—even in church—would serve as a strong deterrent to gun violence.

Examining Gun Carry Laws

Each state sets its own laws to regulate the carrying of firearms in public. These laws determine who can carry guns in public, how they can carry them, and where they can go while armed. Historically, most states prohibited people from carrying guns in public or strongly regulated who could do so. Yet in recent decades, many states have weakened their gun carry laws and have allowed more people to carry guns in public places and have reduced—and, in some cases, eliminated—law enforcement's ability to stop potentially dangerous people from carrying guns in public.

According to a 2017 study published in the *American Journal of Public Health*, an estimated 3 million adult Americans carry a loaded firearm daily. Even more, an estimated 9 million, carry a loaded gun on a monthly basis. Most gun-carrying adults say their primary reason for doing so is for personal protection.

How a person can carry a gun in public depends on state laws. Currently, all states and Washington, DC, allow a person to carry a concealed weapon, a practice called concealed carry. Under concealed carry laws, a person can carry a gun in public either on or near his or her body, such as in a jacket pocket, in a purse, or in a car's glove box.

Thirty-five states require a person to obtain a permit in order to carry a concealed gun in public. The other fifteen states—Alaska, Arizona, Idaho, Kansas, Kentucky, Maine, Mississippi, Missouri, New Hampshire, North Dakota, Oklahoma, South Dakota, Vermont, West Virginia, and Wyoming—allow a person to carry a concealed weapon in public without a permit. Whether the state requires a permit or not, most states have some restrictions on where a person can carry a concealed firearm, such as into bars, schools, hospitals, and public sporting events.

David French, a journalist and Iraq War veteran, carries a concealed gun. His primary motivation for carrying a gun is protection. He explains that he and his family have been threatened online and in person because of their political views. "In just the last five years, we've faced multiple threats—so much so that neighbors have expressed concern for our safety, and theirs," he wrote for *The Atlantic* in 2018. "We've learned the same lesson that so many others have learned. There are evil men in this world, and sometimes they wish you harm." Because of these threats, French has made the choice to carry a gun. "Because of the threats against my family . . . I carry a weapon. My wife does as well. We're not scared. We're prepared,"[31] he writes.

In many states, people are permitted to carry a gun openly in public, a practice called open carry. Open carry allows individuals to keep a gun in easy reach on their body, within a holster or attached to a sling. It does not allow them to carry a gun openly in their

"Because of the threats against my family . . . I carry a weapon. My wife does as well. We're not scared. We're prepared."[31]

—David French, an attorney, journalist, and Iraq War veteran hands. According to data from the Giffords Law Center, only five states and Washington, DC, currently ban open carry of handguns in public places: California, Florida, Illinois, New York, and South Carolina; likewise, California, Florida, Illinois, Massachusetts, Minnesota, and New Jersey also prohibit open carry of long guns. States that allow open carry may require gun owners to obtain a permit to do so. Most also prohibit open carry of guns in certain places, such as schools, state-owned businesses, places where alcohol is served, and on public transportation.

Gun rights advocates argue that allowing people to carry guns in public—whether concealed or open—makes communities safer

Many states permit their residents to openly carry a gun in public. Known as "open carry," the practice allows gun owners to keep a gun attached to a sling or holster so it is within easy reach.

and reduces gun violence. They believe criminals are less likely to act violently if they believe someone nearby is armed. And if criminals do attack, armed citizens are in a better position to defend themselves and others. "We have learned many times over that there is no such thing as a gun free zone. Those with evil intentions will violate the law and carry out their heinous acts no matter what," says Texas state senator Donna Campbell. "It makes no sense to disarm the good guys and leave law-abiding citizens defenseless where violent offenders break the law to do great harm."[32]

In addition, gun rights advocates argue that law-abiding citizens have a Second Amendment right to carry guns in public. After police in Hawaii rejected his application for a license to openly carry a firearm, George Young sued the state for violating his right to carry a gun for protection. In 2018, a three-judge panel on the Ninth Circuit Court of Appeals ruled that Hawaii had overstepped its authority to regulate gun possession outside the home. "We do not take lightly the problem of gun violence," wrote Judge Diarmuid O'Scannlain in the panel's ruling. "But, for better or for worse, the Second Amendment does protect a right to carry a firearm in public for self-defense."[33]

However, others believe that allowing people to carry guns in public only increases the likelihood of gun violence and puts public safety at risk. They believe putting more guns in the public's hands makes it easier for everyday conflicts to escalate into shootings. Some recent studies support this point of view. A 2019 report published in

> "It makes no sense to disarm the good guys and leave law-abiding citizens defenseless where violent offenders break the law to do great harm."[32]
>
> —Donna Campbell, a Texas state senator

> "We do not take lightly the problem of gun violence. But, for better or for worse, the Second Amendment does protect a right to carry a firearm in public for self-defense."[33]
>
> —Diarmuid O'Scannlain, a Ninth Circuit Court of Appeals judge

the *Journal of Empirical Legal Studies* found that states that implemented a right-to-carry handgun law experienced a 13 to 15 percent increase in violent crime ten years after the law's adoption. Stanford University law professor John J. Donohue, who led the study, notes,

> Whatever benefit might come from gun carrying by private citizens seems to be more than offset by overall increases in violent crime. A number of recent studies have found that permissive gun carrying leads to higher rates of homicide and there is little question it leads to enormous increases in gun thefts that can further stimulate criminal activity. Indeed, while gun carrying has shown no ability to reduce robberies, states that adopt right to carry laws see *increases* in the percentage of robberies committed with a gun.[34]

Arming Teachers at School

In the wake of school shootings, gun rights advocates have called for teachers in the country's schools to be armed with guns. They believe having armed teachers would deter shooters from entering schools. In the event a shooter did enter a school, armed teachers would be able to move quickly to stop the shooter and minimize injuries and deaths.

Some states have already passed legislation to allow teachers to carry guns at school. In 2019, Florida's governor signed a law that allows the state's teachers to carry guns. The law expands the state's existing Guardian Program, which was passed in 2018 and permits some school staffers to carry guns at school. The expanded law allows teachers to be armed in the classroom. Teachers volunteer and must pass a background check and psychiatric evaluation and attend a gun-safety training course with a local sheriff's office. Sheriff Bob Gualtieri of Pinellas County supports arming teachers and staff in schools and urges Florida's school districts to

participate in the state's Guardian Program. "Seconds matter when stopping an active shooter and the Commission urges you to maximize the authority you have under current Florida law to enhance school safety by permitting additional qualified and willing personnel to be voluntarily armed to protect our children from harm,"[35] Gualtieri wrote in a letter to Florida's school superintendents.

The Okeechobee School District voted in July 2019 to arm teachers and other school staff in the classroom. Volunteers will go through 144 hours of training, undergo psychological and drug testing, and have their guns inspected. One teacher who has volunteered feels ready for the added responsibility in the classroom. "Twenty years as a teacher, you know your kids, you wouldn't want to see anything bad happen to any of them," the teacher says. "For me, the pros definitely outweighed the cons. You know you have to be ready and prepared if something happens. You have to be willing to do what needs to be done."[36]

Carrying Guns in Public Protects Citizens

Todd Blodgett is a gun rights activist who argues that Americans should be allowed to carry guns in public nationwide:

Violent crime tends to drop in states that enact concealed-carry laws. I imagine that's because even thugs prefer breathing to being blown away. I hold concealed-carry permits issued by Iowa and Utah, and nearly always carry a loaded handgun—usually, a .380 pocket pistol. I've not been victimized since I began carrying. Before that, though, I was hospitalized for two weeks in Washington, D.C., after being brutally mugged. A loaded gun aimed at violent perpetrators facilitates an instant attitude adjustment, and law-abiding, innocent U.S. citizens should be able to protect—with deadly force, if necessary—their lives, property, and the lives of others. . . . With 50-state concealed-carry, some carjackers, muggers, rapists, would-be killers, home invaders and other violence-prone perps, will likely be snuffed out by their intended victims. But where's the downside? Not all violence is bad, and permanently retiring such vicious reprobates would be good riddance.

Todd Blodgett, "Trump's Proposed Concealed-Carry Law Will Reduce Crime, Protect Americans," *Des Moines (IA) Register*, January 2, 2019. www.desmoinesregister.com.

However, not all educators favor arming teachers in the classroom. A March 2018 survey of nearly five hundred teachers found that 73 percent oppose arming school staff. In Florida, none of the state's largest school districts has approved the program. "Teachers have a lot on their plates," says Tamara Shamburger, chair of the Hillsborough County school board, which voted against arming teachers. "Their focus has to be on educating their kids and not fighting off bad guys."[37] Fedrick Ingram, president of the Florida Education Association, also opposes arming

"Teachers have a lot on their plates. Their focus has to be on educating their kids and not fighting off bad guys."[37]

—Tamara Shamburger, the chair of Florida's Hillsborough County school board

Carrying Guns in Public Puts Citizens at Risk

Nina Vinik, a program director for gun violence prevention at the Joyce Foundation, argues that allowing guns in public increases the risk of gun violence in America:

> There is ample evidence of gun owners feeling overconfident about their ability to use guns responsibly, leading to riskier behavior and outcomes ranging from criminal misconduct and gun accidents to lost or stolen guns. Right-to-carry laws also normalize the practice of carrying guns, making it harder for the police to know who is and who is not allowed to possess guns in public. Examples abound of concealed-gun carriers attempting—and failing—to thwart crimes, often with deadly consequences. Last year in Portland, Ore., Portland State University campus police officers arrived as a "good Samaritan" with a concealed carry permit was trying to break up a fight. The police saw the gun held by the permit holder—a Navy veteran, postal worker and father of three—and in the confusion shot and killed him. . . . With gun-related deaths topping nearly 40,000 in 2017 in the U.S., according to federal data, anyone who is seriously considering carrying a gun for self-protection would do well to consider the evidence.

Nina Vinik, "Concealed Carry Doesn't Guarantee Our Safety—It Puts Us at Greater Risk," *Chicago Tribune*, January 16, 2019. www.chicagotribune.com.

VIEWPOINT

teachers at school because it burdens teachers with an enormous responsibility and could put students in more danger if a student were able to get a gun that was left unguarded. In addition, Ingram believes that arming teachers takes resources away from real solutions to school shootings and gun violence. "What we know is that arming teachers in the state of Florida is not a real solution," Ingram says. "We should be talking about mental health, we should be talking about school counselors, we should be talking about a psychiatrist, and we should be talking about the funding that it takes to actually make our schools safer."[38]

Many worry that arming teachers will bring additional dangers into the classroom. According to a 2019 analysis by the Giffords Law Center, there were seventy-four publicly reported incidents in which guns were mishandled at school over the previous five years. In one incident, a teacher unintentionally fired a gun in class during a safety demonstration. In another, a loaded gun fell out of a teacher's waistband on the school playground.

Stand-Your-Ground Laws

When people carry guns in public, there is debate on how they can and should be used. Most states have laws that allow a person to respond to a threat of physical injury with force. Most of these self-defense laws state that the person being threatened has a duty to retreat. If that individual retreats but the threat continues, that person can defend himself or herself with force. In some states, however, "stand-your-ground" laws allow a person who feels threatened to use deadly force immediately, without first attempting to retreat or get away.

As of 2019, twenty-five states have enacted some form of stand-your-ground laws, according to the National Conference of State Legislatures. Supporters of these laws say they give people the right to protect themselves. In 2015, Jeb Bush, the former governor of Florida, defended the law at the NRA's annual meeting. "In Florida you can defend yourself anywhere you have a legal right to be," he said. "You shouldn't have to choose between being attacked and going to jail."[39]

Those who oppose stand-your-ground laws argue that they encourage average people to become armed vigilantes, which threatens public safety. According to the Giffords Law Center, multiple studies have shown that Florida's stand-your-ground law has increased violence. The law's implementation was associated with a 32 percent increase in firearm homicide rates and a 24 percent increase in overall homicide rates. In addition, in 79 percent of Florida's stand-your-ground cases, the shooter could have retreated to avoid the deadly confrontation, and in 68 percent of the cases, the person killed was unarmed.

Use of these laws has sparked controversy. In July 2018, Markeis McGlockton and Michael Drejka got into an altercation over a parking space outside a convenience store in Clearwater, Florida. After McGlockton shoved Drejka to the ground, Drejka drew his gun and fatally shot McGlockton in the chest. At first, police said that Florida's stand-your-ground law prevented them from arresting Drejka because he feared further harm after McGlockton had violently shoved him. Florida's law states that victims are justified in using deadly force if they reasonably believe that it is necessary to prevent imminent death or great bodily harm or to prevent a forcible felony crime. The law does not require victims to retreat if they are not committing a crime and are in a place where they have a right to be.

The decision triggered outcry from many in the community and calls for reform to Florida's law. Civil rights attorney Benjamin Crump also called for Drejka's prosecution. "The state attorney needs to make sure this cold-blooded murderer does not get away with this," Crump says. "It's the law, and it's ludicrous. It's just a very bad law that encourages people in society to take the laws into their own hands."[40] Eventually, prosecutors decided that Drejka was not protected by the state's stand-your-ground law and arrested him. Drejka was charged with manslaughter and was convicted in 2019; he was sentenced to twenty years in jail.

Protect or Endanger?

The role of guns in public has sparked intense debate among gun rights supporters and gun control advocates. Gun rights supporters argue that putting guns in the hands of law-abiding citizens deters and prevents gun violence. They want teachers and school staff to be armed in the event of a school shooting. Yet others believe that adding more guns to public places and schools will have the opposite effect and lead to even more incidents of gun violence.

CHAPTER FIVE

Treating Gun Violence as a Public Health Issue

Every day, nearly one hundred people are killed with guns in the United States, according to the American Psychological Association. Some commit suicide, and others are victims of domestic or community violence. Guns are lethal weapons and are often used on impulse. People in crisis who have guns are more likely to succeed the first time they attempt to harm themselves or others.

For young Americans, the statistics are even more concerning. Gun-related injuries are the second-leading cause of childhood death in the United States. In 2016, guns killed more than thirty-one hundred children and teens, according to a 2018 study by University of Michigan researchers. That translates to about eight children being killed every day by a gun. American youth are also more likely to die from gun injuries, at a rate that is thirty-six times higher than the average rate for youth living in twelve other wealthy countries. In fact, gun-related deaths kill more American youth than cancer, heart disease, and other infections and disorders.

Because gun-related injuries and deaths have become so prevalent, public health and medical professionals are increasingly calling for gun violence to be treated as a public health issue. "Gun violence is a major public health problem and a leading cause of death in this country and we need to do something about it,"[41] says Ali Rowhani-Rahbar, an adjunct associate professor of pediatrics at the University of Washington. There are a number of ideas on the best way to approach gun violence, including by devoting more resources to research, implementing individual measures to identify and treat those at risk, and adopting community-based programs to reduce gun violence.

"Gun violence is a major public health problem and a leading cause of death in this country and we need to do something about it."[41]

—Ali Rowhani-Rahbar, an adjunct associate professor of pediatrics at the University of Washington

Increase Funding for Research

Many public health experts and scientists believe that to reduce gun violence, the United States needs to devote more funding and research to the issue. Rebecca Cunningham, director of the University of Michigan Injury Prevention Center and lead author of

In the United States, gun-related injuries are the second-leading cause of childhood death—and eight children are killed every day by a gun.

a gun violence study, agrees that more research needs to be done to prevent and reduce gun violence. "We have dozens of teams of scientists and clinicians working on prevention and treatment of pediatric cancers, congenital conditions and heart diseases, conditions where death rates have also fallen," she says. "We hope these data help put firearm deaths of young people in the proper context, so we can study and test potential preventive measures while respecting the Second Amendment rights of gun owners."[42]

In the United States, the CDC is the leading public health agency that strives to save lives and protect the health of all Americans. Across the country, the CDC leads many programs and research efforts to save and improve lives. In recent years, the CDC has focused on public health issues such as alcohol-related harms, food safety, motor vehicle injury, heart disease and stroke, HIV, obesity, and more.

Yet even though gun violence is a leading cause of death for Americans, particularly youth, there is little federally funded research being performed on gun violence and ways to reduce it, unlike other public health issues such as smoking or cancer. According to a 2017 study published in the *Journal of the American Medical Association*, gun violence research received only 5.3 percent of the federal research funding that research into motor vehicle accidents received, even though they kill similar numbers of Americans every year. "We know far less about gun violence as a cause of injury and death than we do about almost every medical problem,"[43] says Dr. Elinore Kaufman, the chief resident in surgery at New York–Presbyterian/ Weill Cornell Medical Center.

The Dickey Amendment is one of the main reasons why there is a lack of federally funded research on gun violence. The amendment, which

"We know far less about gun violence as a cause of injury and death than we do about almost every medical problem."[43]

—Dr. Elinore Kaufman, the chief resident in surgery at New York–Presbyterian/Weill Cornell Medical Center

Cure Violence Programs

Based in Chicago, Cure Violence (CV) programs treat gun violence as a communicable disease. According to the program's website, "Exposure to violence has been scientifically shown to increase a person's risk of adopting violent behavior themselves, meaning that violent behavior transmits and spreads based on exposure—just like an epidemic disease." The program works in three phases. First, violence interrupters, who are often members of the community, identify potentially violent conflicts and mediate them to a peaceful solution. Then, outreach workers identify those most at risk of violence and connect them to community services to help them make positive life changes, such as education, employment, and counseling. The third element of the CV program involves educating the public to change social norms around the use of violence. The program encourages community leaders to speak out for positive change and reducing violence.

Reviews of CV programs have found that using the CV model has significantly reduced the rates of gun violence. A 2014 evaluation of four Chicago police districts where CV programs were implemented reported a 31 percent drop in gun homicides, a 7 percent decrease in total violent crime, and a 19 percent decline in shootings. These results show that CV programs can be an effective way to reduce gun violence in targeted neighborhoods.

Cure Violence, "The Big Idea." https://cvg.org.

was part of a 1996 congressional spending provision, bans the CDC and other federal agencies from funding research that could be viewed as advocating gun control.

There are signs the federal government has begun to recognize gun violence as a public health issue that would benefit from more research. In December 2019, President Donald Trump signed a spending bill that included $25 million for the CDC and the National Institutes of Health to conduct research on gun violence. "With this investment, the best public health researchers in the country will be put to work to identify ways to reduce injury and death due to firearms,"[44] says House representative Nita Lowey.

Identifying Risk Factors

Public health experts hope that more research into gun violence may help them better identify and understand the risk factors that lead to gun violence. They know that a complex variety of risk and protective factors make people more or less likely to use a firearm to harm themselves or others. For this reason, there is no single profile that can accurately predict who will use a gun for violence. However, there are some risk factors that have been identified as making people more likely to commit a violent act with a gun.

A history of substance abuse and past violent behavior, especially domestic violence, are strongly linked to gun violence. According to a report from the Consortium for Risk-Based Firearm Policy, substance abuse, particularly alcohol abuse, is a major risk factor that increases the likelihood that a person will use a

Gun violence experts stress that substance abuse, especially alcohol abuse, vastly increases the likelihood that someone will use a gun to commit a violent act.

gun to commit a violent act. "The best predictor of future risky or violent behavior is past behavior," says Beth McGinty, an associate professor at the Johns Hopkins Bloomberg School of Public Health who was involved with the report. "Having multiple DUIs or DWIs [offenses for driving under the influence or driving while intoxicated] is one way of operationalizing that type of risk." In addition, the report found that a history of domestic violence or violent misdemeanors was also linked to gun violence. "If you want to screen for factors that might indicate people who are at high risk of committing gun violence, it's these factors that suggest risk factors for future violence,"[45] McGinty says.

Having access to a gun, along with certain personality traits, is another risk factor for gun violence. According to a 2019 study from the University of Texas Medical Branch, people who have access to a gun are more than eighteen times as likely to threaten someone as someone who does not have gun access. In addition, personality traits such as impulsivity and excessive anger can make a person who has access to a gun more likely to use it in a violent act. Researchers also found that people who were more likely to be hostile were more than three times more likely to threaten another person with a gun.

Mental illness has long been blamed by some people for gun violence. After the mass shootings in Dayton and El Paso in 2019, Trump spoke to the nation and stated that "mental illness and hatred pull the trigger, not the gun."[46] However, mental health experts argue that the vast majority of people suffering from mental illness are not inherently violent. "Those who suffer from mental illness—be it depression, anxiety, bipolar disorder, or other issues—are generally not inclined to harm others,"[47] says Dr. Carla Marie Manly, a clinical psychologist. According to the American Psychological Association, people with serious mental illnesses commit only about 3 percent of violent crimes. "Blaming mental illness for the gun violence in our country is simplistic and inaccurate and goes against the scientific evidence currently available,"[48] says Arthur C. Evans Jr., the association's chief executive officer.

Individual Interventions

Some people believe that the best way to reduce gun violence is to implement programs and interventions to assess and treat individuals at risk of violence. At the individual level, mental health treatment and behavioral threat assessments can work to identify those at risk of violence and help them find alternative solutions to problems that do not involve harming themselves or others.

Although mental health experts emphasize that most people suffering from a mental illness are neither dangerous nor violent, some who are experiencing suicidal thoughts or feelings of desperation can be at increased risk of violence. Making mental health treatment available to all who need it can often prevent gun violence. "We need to invest in mentally healthy communities—communities that invest in reducing the drivers of psychological pain and suffering while increasing drivers of belonging, connection, compassion, and purpose," says Michelle G. Paul, a clinical psychologist. "Pain and suffering begets negative and sometimes aggressive behaviors toward self and others."[49]

Behavioral threat assessment programs are another way to identify and help individuals who are in crisis before they escalate into violence. These programs, which can be implemented in schools, workplaces, and communities, use trained teams to identify individuals and recognize the signs that a person is in crisis. The team assesses the person to determine how serious the threat is and develops a plan to intervene and address the underlying problem or crisis that is causing the person's behavior before violence occurs.

Community Intervention Programs

At the community level, several intervention programs have shown promise in reducing gun violence in local communities. Some community initiatives focus on early childhood and aim to help parents raise emotionally healthy children. Other programs intervene with individuals in crisis who are threatening violence. Other programs involve public health messages about respon-

Gun Violence Is an Epidemic

In the eyes of some, gun violence is much more than a political issue. It has become an epidemic. Cardiologist David Skorton, who is the president and chief executive officer of the Association of American Medical Colleges, warns against the spreading crisis of gun violence:

> From the perspective of the medical community, gun violence is not primarily a political or ideological issue. With 100 people in America dying of gun violence each day, the equivalent of multiple mass shootings, seven days a week, it's a public health crisis. It's an epidemic. It's relentless, and it's spreading. Our nation's EMTs, emergency room clinicians and trauma specialists deal every day with these horrific acts of violence—trying, often in vain, to save lives and repair shattered bodies. Even many of the victims who survive will be burdened by the physical and psychological trauma for the rest of their lives, along with first responders, families and entire communities.

David Skorton, "Gun Violence Is a Health Crisis, Not a Political Football. It's Time to Act: Cardiologist," *USA Today*, September 10, 2019. www.usatoday.com.

sible gun ownership, including safe gun storage to prevent unauthorized access to guns.

One type of program, called Group Violence Intervention (GVI), has been successfully implemented in several cities. The GVI strategy was first used in Operation Ceasefire in Boston during the 1990s, which targeted youth gun violence and resulted in a 61 percent reduction in youth homicides. GVI is based on the idea that in most cities, a small but identifiable segment of the community is responsible for the largest share of gun violence. These individuals are often linked to groups that compete in a violent rivalry with other groups, which results in most of a neighborhood's gun violence.

GVI programs gather respected community members, including faith leaders, social service providers, researchers, and law enforcement officials. Together, this group identifies the people in the community who are most at risk of committing or becoming the

Group violence intervention programs identify people in a community who are most at risk of committing gun violence or becoming the victims of gun violence, and then begin a series of in-person meetings with these individuals.

victims of gun violence. Then they begin a series of small group, in-person meetings with these individuals. The purpose of the meeting is to clearly communicate that the gun violence must end. The message comes from the community's moral leaders, such as clergy, victims of gun violence, parents of victims, and reformed violent offenders. Law enforcement respectfully informs the individuals that swift legal action will be taken against any group or individual responsible for new acts of violence. This process continues until the targeted individuals understand that the community is asking for the police to get involved in any future shootings. This creates a focused deterrence effect that has been shown to reduce violent behavior.

During the meetings, the at-risk individuals are put in contact with social service providers who can help them access resources they need to turn their lives around. These resources include tutoring so they can earn a general equivalency diploma (GED), transportation assistance, mental health treatment, housing support, and more. The program recognizes that meeting a person's basic needs can reduce the likelihood that they will engage in violent behavior. According to the Giffords Law Center, GVI programs have reduced homicide rates by 30 to 60 percent in several cities.

The Hospital-Based Violence Intervention Program

Another community-based strategy to reduce gun violence focuses on high-risk individuals who have been admitted to a hospital for a serious injury from violence. This type of program, called a hospital-based violence intervention program (HVIP), is based on the idea that the greatest risk factor for gun violence is a history of previous violence and violent injury. In fact, having a violent injury makes a person twice as likely to die in the future from violent injury, according to the Giffords Law Center. In addition, being a victim of violence also increases a person's likelihood of committing violent acts themselves. HVIP relies on the idea that when hospitalized for a violent, serious injury, a person is more open to positive intervention. Screening identifies candidates and connects them with a trained case manager. The case manager gives these individuals oversight and help while in the hospital and in the months after release. During this time, case managers help connect individuals with community organizations to help them get the services they need, such as mental health services, tattoo removal, GED programs, employment, legal advice and advocacy, and housing. In addition, because HVIP case managers come from similar backgrounds as their clients, they are better able to personally connect with them.

YouthAlive!, a nonprofit organization based in Oakland, California, is one of the pioneers of the HVIP strategy. Under its Caught in the Crossfire program, YouthAlive! uses trained interventional specialists to reach young people recovering from violent injuries. Specialists help clients connect to community services and provide home-based mentoring and long-term case management and assistance.

One Goal

Treating gun violence as a public health issue can incorporate a variety of programs, interventions, and assessments. All depend on the involvement of the community, government, medical professionals, and law enforcement. Agreeing on effective strategies is difficult, but many view the challenge as a necessary effort to help save lives. While proposals range from increasing research to implementing intervention programs, the goal is the same: stopping gun-related deaths and injuries.

Introduction: Dying from Gun Violence

1. Quoted in Jim Schaefer and Tresa Baldas, "Inside the El Paso Shooting: A Store Manager, a Frantic Father, Grateful Survivors," *USA Today*, August 10, 2019. www.usatoday.com.
2. Quoted in Schaefer and Baldas, "Inside the El Paso Shooting."
3. Quoted in Institute for Health Metrics and Evaluation, "Six Countries in the Americas Account for Half of All Firearm Deaths," University of Washington, August 28, 2018. www.healthdata.org.
4. Quoted in Melissa Howell, "Activists Demand Change in DC During Nationwide Rally to End Gun Violence," WTOP News, August 17, 2019. https://wtop.com.

Chapter One: Should Assault-Style Weapons Be Banned?

5. Joe Biden, "Banning Assault Weapons Works," *New York Times*, August 11, 2019. www.nytimes.com.
6. Quoted in Peter Dujardin, "'Assault' Rifles vs. Handguns: Which Are the Bigger Problem?," *Newport News (VA) Daily Press*, March 21, 2018. www.dailypress.com.
7. Quoted in Alex Yablon, "Diving Into the Data on Assault Weapons Bans," The Trace, August 16, 2019. www.thetrace.org.
8. Quoted in Christopher Ingraham, "It's Time to Bring Back the Assault Weapons Ban, Gun Violence Experts Say," *Washington Post*, February 15, 2018. www.washingtonpost.com.
9. Quoted in United States Senator for California: Dianne Feinstein, "Senators Introduce Assault Weapons Ban," press release, January 9, 2019. www.feinstein.senate.gov.
10. Quoted in Sheryl Gay Stolberg, "Divided Democrats Step Back from Assault Weapons Ban," *New York Times*, September 11, 2019. www.nytimes.com.
11. Quoted in Christina Maxouris, "The Gilroy Festival Shooter Bought His Rifle in Nevada. 'I Can't Put Borders Up . . . in a Neighboring State,' Governor Says," CNN, July 30, 2019. www.cnn.com.

12. Quoted in Jesse J. Smith, "Massive Noncompliance with SAFE Act," *Hudson Valley One*, July 7, 2016. https://hudson valleyone.com.

Chapter Two: Should Universal Background Checks Be Required for All Gun Purchases?

13. Quoted in Manny Fernandez et al., "Texas Shooting Leaves 7 Dead and at Least 21 Injured Near Odessa," *New York Times*, August 31, 2019. www.nytimes.com.
14. Quoted in John C. Moritz, "Gov. Abbott Laments Failed Background Check for the Gunman Who Killed 7 in Odessa, Texas," *Corpus Christi (TX) Caller Times*, September 2, 2019. www.caller.com.
15. Quoted in Jordain Carney, "Schumer: Odessa Shooting 'Could Have Been Avoided' with Background Check Bill," *The Hill* (Washington, DC), September 3, 2019. https://thehill.com.
16. Quoted in Greg St. Martin, "New Study Finds 1 in 5 Gun Owners Obtained Firearm Without Background Check," Northeastern University, January 5, 2017. https://news.northeastern .edu.
17. Quoted in School of Public Health, "Universal Background Checks Lower Homicide Rates," Boston University, March 28, 2019. www.bu.edu.
18. Quoted in Lois Beckett, "Gun Laws That Cost Millions Had Little Effect Because They Weren't Enforced," *The Guardian* (Manchester, UK), October 13, 2017. www.theguardian.com.
19. Quoted in Beckett, "Gun Laws That Cost Millions Had Little Effect Because They Weren't Enforced."
20. Quoted in John Bresnahan, "House Passes Most Sweeping Gun Control Legislation in Decades," Politico, February 27, 2019. www.politico.com.
21. Quoted in Bresnahan, "House Passes Most Sweeping Gun Control Legislation in Decades."

Chapter Three: Should the Government Expand Gun Ownership Regulations?

22. Quoted in Sean Gregory and Chris Wilson, "6 Real Ways We Can Reduce Gun Violence in America," *Time*, March 22, 2018. www.time.com.

23. Cassandra K. Crifasi et al., *The Impact of Handgun Purchaser Licensing on Gun Violence*. Baltimore, MD: Johns Hopkins Center for Gun Policy and Research, Bloomberg School of Public Health, 2019. www.jhsph.edu.

24. Chelsea Parsons et al., *Hate and Guns: A Terrifying Combination*. Washington, DC: Center for American Progress, 2016. https://cdn.americanprogress.org.

25. Quoted in Chris Eger, "California Passes Bill to Take Guns from Those in the 'Hate Crime Loophole,'" Guns.com, September 13, 2017. www.guns.com.

26. Quoted in Congressman David Cicilline, "Cicilline's Disarm Hate Act Heads to House Floor," press release, September 10, 2019. https://cicilline.house.gov.

27. Quoted in Melanie Sevcenko, "'Boyfriend Loophole': Backlash After Oregon Joins 23 States in Curbing Guns," *The Guardian* (Manchester, UK), March 21, 2018. www.theguardian.com.

28. Quoted in Sevcenko, "'Boyfriend Loophole.'"

29. Quoted in Dareh Gregorian, "'Red Flag' Laws Could Reduce Gun Violence—but Not How Some Lawmakers Say," NBC News, August 13, 2019. www.nbcnews.com.

Chapter Four: Should Americans Be Able to Carry Guns in Public?

30. Quoted in CBS DFW, "Officials: 3 Dead, Including Gunman, Following Fatal Church Shooting in White Settlement," December 29, 2019. https://dfw.cbslocal.com.

31. David French, "What Critics Don't Understand About Gun Culture," *The Atlantic*, February 27, 2018. www.theatlantic.com.

32. Quoted in Texas Senate, "Sen. Campbell Files SB 535 to Secure Texans' Right to Carry in Church," January 30, 2019. https://senate.texas.gov.

33. Quoted in Reuters, "U.S. Appeals Court Upholds Right to Carry Gun in Public," July 24, 2018. www.reuters.com.

34. John J. Donohue, "Stanford Law's John Donohue on Mass Shootings and Gun Regulation in the U.S.," Stanford Law School, August 6, 2019. https://law.stanford.edu.

35. Quoted in Jeffrey Schweers, "Pinellas Sheriff Urges Florida Superintendents to Adopt Guardian Program, Arm School Personnel," *Tallahassee (FL) Democrat*, March 13, 2019. www.tallahassee.com.

36. Quoted in Elina Shirazi, "Florida Begins Arming Teachers as Large School Districts Rebuff Controversial Program," Fox News, October 9, 2019. www.foxnews.com.

37. Quoted in Arian Campo-Flores, "Florida Decided to Let Teachers Carry Guns but Few Are," *Wall Street Journal*, September 9, 2019. www.wsj.com.

38. Quoted in Katie Mettler, "It's the Law Now: In Florida, Teachers Can Carry Guns at School," *Washington Post*, May 9, 2019. www.washingtonpost.com.

39. Quoted in Elizabeth Elkin and Dakin Andone, "What You Need to Know About 'Stand Your Ground' Laws," CNN, July 29, 2018. www.cnn.com.

40. Quoted in Jason Hanna and Eliott C. McLaughlin, "Push Doesn't Justify Shooting, Slain Man's Father Says of 'Stand Your Ground' Case," CNN, July 26, 2018. www.cnn.com.

Chapter Five: Treating Gun Violence as a Public Health Issue

41. Quoted in Colin Poitras, "Public Health Critical to Addressing Gun Violence Epidemic," Yale School of Medicine, November 30, 2018. https://medicine.yale.edu.

42. Quoted in Kara Gavin, "How Children, Teens Die in America: Study Reveals Widespread, Persistent Role of Firearms," Michigan News, University of Michigan, December 19, 2018. https://news.umich.edu.

43. Quoted in Sean Gregory and Chris Wilson, "6 Real Ways We Can Reduce Gun Violence in America," *Time*, March 22, 2018. https://time.com.

44. Quoted in Veronica Stracqualursi, "Congress Agrees to Millions in Gun Violence Research for the First Time in Decades," CNN, December 17, 2019. www.cnn.com.

45. Quoted in Kaitlyn Sullivan, "Mental Illness Isn't a Major Risk Factor for Gun Violence, but Here's What Is," NBC News, August 6, 2019. www.nbcnews.com.

46. Quoted in Jonathan Allen, "In Tragic Self-Owns, Trump Denounces Racism, and Calls for Immigration Reform," NBC News, August 5, 2019. www.nbcnews.com.
47. Quoted in Healthline, "Social Contagion, Not Mental Illness, Fuels Gun Violence," 2019. www.healthline.com.
48. Quoted in American Psychological Association, "Statement of APA CEO on Gun Violence and Mental Health," press release, August 5, 2019. www.apa.org.
49. Quoted in Healthline, "Social Contagion, Not Mental Illness, Fuels Gun Violence."

Brady Campaign—www.bradyunited.org

The Brady Campaign is one of the oldest gun control organizations in America. Its website has information about gun violence issues, fact sheets, legislation, litigation, reports, statistics, and more.

Coalition to Stop Gun Violence—www.csgv.org

The Coalition to Stop Gun Violence strives to reduce gun violence through policy development, advocacy, community engagement, and effective training. Its website has information about gun violence issues, information on how to take action, blog posts, and media releases.

Everytown for Gun Safety—https://everytown.org

Everytown is a movement of Americans working together to end gun violence and build safer communities. Its website has information about gun violence issues, how to organize a student group, and events protesting gun violence across the country.

Giffords Law Center to Prevent Gun Violence
https://lawcenter.giffords.org

The Giffords Law Center is a leading policy organization dedicated to saving lives from gun violence. Its website has a multitude of resources, including fact sheets, statistics, policy papers, and more regarding gun issues and laws.

Gun Owners of America—https://gunowners.org

Gun Owners of America is a nonprofit lobbying organization formed to defend the Second Amendment rights of gun owners. Its website includes gun fact sheets, links to articles, and press releases related to the organization's activities and various gun rights topics.

Gun Violence Archive—www.gunviolencearchive.org

This is an independent research group that maintains an on-line archive. It collects data on gun violence incidents from over seventy-five hundred law enforcement, media, government, and commercial sources daily. The archive provides near–real time data about the results of gun violence.

National Rifle Association (NRA)—https://home.nra.org

The NRA is a gun rights advocacy group in the United States. Its website has information about and links to a wide variety of issues, events, programs, membership, and more.

Books

John Allen, *School Shootings and Violence*. San Diego: ReferencePoint, 2019.

Tiffanie Drayton, *Coping with Gun Violence*. New York: Rosen, 2019.

Natalie Hyde, *Gun Violence*. New York: Crabtree, 2019.

Michelle Roehm McCann, *Enough Is Enough: How Students Can Join the Fight for Gun Safety*. New York: Simon Pulse, 2019.

Bradley Steffens, *Gun Violence and Mass Shootings*. San Diego: ReferencePoint, 2019.

Internet Sources

Chad Brooks, "The Second Amendment & the Right to Bear Arms," Live Science, June 28, 2017. www.livescience.com.

Center for American Progress, "Assault Weapons and High-Capacity Magazines Must Be Banned," August 12, 2019. www.americanprogress.org.

Nate Cohn and Margot Sanger-Katz, "On Guns, Public Opinion and Public Policy Often Diverge," *New York Times*, August 10, 2019. www.nytimes.com.

John Gramlich, "What the Data Says About Gun Deaths in the U.S.," Pew Research Center, August 16, 2019. www.pewresearch.org.

John Gramlich and Katherine Schaeffer, "Facts About Guns in the United States," Pew Research Center, October 22, 2019. www.pewresearch.org.

Benjy Sarlin, "6 Proposals to Reduce Gun Violence and How They Work," *USA Today*, February 28, 2018. www.nbcnews.com.

ABOUT THE AUTHOR

Carla Mooney is the author of many books for young adults and children. She lives in Pittsburgh, Pennsylvania, with her husband and three children.